31 DAYS WITH THE VIRTUES

31 DAYS WITH THE VIRTUES

N. KARL HADEN, PH.D. & ROB JENKINS

Printed in the United States of America

Cover design by Daniel Ojedokun

Library of Congress Cataloging-in-Publications data is available upon request.

ISBN 978-1-947309-31-9

Books are available in quantity for promotional or premium use. For information, email info@deedspublishing.com.

First Edition, 2020

10 9 8 7 6 5 4 3 2 1

In appreciation to the countless leaders with whom the Academy for Advancing Leadership has had the privilege of working.

INTRODUCTION

While this little book is a sequel to *The 9 Virtues of Exceptional Leaders*, one can also read it as an extended introduction. *31 Days with the Virtues, Practicing the Habits of Exceptional Leaders* introduces the reader to both the concept of virtue and each of the Nine Virtues discussed in our preceding book. We have taken quotations from *The 9 Virtues* as starting points for reflection. Four of the 31 days consider a general aspect of virtuous leadership, while three days are devoted to each of the Nine Virtues. Rather than addressing a single virtue three days in a row, we have spread the virtues across 31 days.

We continue to hold fast to the belief that knowledge about leadership is insufficient to make a person an exceptional leader. While a level of understanding should precede every action, we put the accent on action—on the practice of leadership. Moreover, we contend that certain types of practices, when they become habits, form the best leaders. These habits are the virtues of exceptional leaders.

In his *Nicomachean Ethics*, Aristotle, the father of virtue ethics, defines virtue as "a state of character concerned with a choice, lying in a mean, that is, the mean that is relative to us, this being determined by a rational principle, and by that principle by which the man [or woman] of practical wisdom would determine it."[1] While this lengthy definition merits an exhaustive explanation, we wish only to highlight several considerations relevant to virtuous leadership:

- Virtue is about action — choices we make. When we make the same choice in the same circumstances over and over again, the choice becomes a habit. Habits promoting the well-being of self and others are virtues; those harming us and others are vices.

- Habits define and shape character. When we make a choice, when we act, we are not just doing something, we are becoming someone. We know today from neuroscience what Aristotle could only surmise: habits — virtues and vices — become hardwired in our brains.

- Knowing the right action to take requires practical wisdom—or what is sometimes called prudence. More specifically, if we want to know the right action to take, we should do what the person of practical wisdom would do.

---

1. Aristotle. *Nicomachean Ethics.* Trans. by W.D. Ross. Stilwell, KS: Digireads. com Publishing, 2005. Book I.

We believe Aristotle's person of practical wisdom is analogous to the exceptional leader. Exceptional leaders habitually act to promote the well-being of the people and organizations they lead. These moral exemplars teach us by example the right action to take. They are role models showing us what we ought and ought not do.

By our definition, the exceptional leader is the virtuous leader. But, as readers have reminded us many times since the publication of *The 9 Virtues*, not all leaders are virtuous. What makes virtuous leaders different? Here are four distinguishing characteristics:

1. **They promote human flourishing.** Leadership, like the virtues themselves, has one aim: to promote human flourishing. Virtuous leaders create environments where people can thrive through having a sense of purpose and opportunities to learn, grow, and contribute. This aim of virtuous leadership is not a substitute for the profit motive or the drive for institutional excellence. Rather, profit and excellence become the means to the goal of promoting human flourishing.

2. **They take moral responsibility.** As noted above, virtuous leadership is rooted in ethics. Virtuous leaders appreciate, understand, and act for the welfare of others. The work of the virtuous leader is moral work, work based on a set of

principles, beliefs, and values about what is right for the organizations and people in it. Such leaders see their efforts not only as a privilege but as a duty. Like a fiduciary responsibility, virtuous leaders embrace the covenant of trust granted to them by their followers.

3. **They build character.** Three questions are fundamental for any leader. First, "What do I need to know?" Second, since leaders are judged by the decisions they make, the question, "What should I do?" combines knowledge with action. Good leaders will also ask themselves and others, "Why should I do this?" But exceptional leaders, virtuous leaders, ask a fourth question: "What kind of person should I be?" As the Stoic Zeno of Citium (334-262 BCE) observed, "The fountain of life is character. And, from it, in their order, flow forth our actions."

4. **They serve as exemplars.** Virtue ethics are unique in that they are based not on rules or systems but on exemplars, paradigmatic individuals who show us how we should think and act. We can learn much about leadership from reading and life experiences, but virtuous leadership emphasizes mentoring, role modeling, and studying the lives of those worthy of emulation. Recognizing the duty of leadership and the importance of character-building, virtuous leaders are com-

mitted to passing their wisdom on to others to develop exceptional leaders throughout the organization and beyond.

Many of us have heard that 21 days are required to form a new habit. Over the past few decades, researchers have shown this assumption is false. From genetics to upbringing and the environment, and from simple behaviors to complicated ones, numerous factors affect the time required to form new habits. There is nothing scientific in our 31-day approach. Our goal was to write an accessible meditation for each day of the month.

31 Days is easily read from cover to cover, but to do so is to miss the point of it. While the selections are quickly read, we hope they linger long on the mind. They are, after all, reflections. We hope the reader will take one day at a time, perhaps five to 10 minutes in the early morning or in the evening to prepare for the next day, to read and meditate on the quotation and the corresponding reflection. Each day's reflection ends with an idea for practicing the virtue. Whether you take our suggested practice or think of another, the goal is always action. The virtues of exceptional leaders are habits, but like the habits of a virtuoso, they result from deliberate practice.

N. Karl Haden, Ph.D.
Rob Jenkins
November 2019

TABLE OF CONTENTS

31 DAYS WITH THE VIRTUES

VIRTUES & VICES
(virtue)

Virtue is excellence in character: character shaped by actions into habitual ways of thinking and acting.

"Excellence" is essentially a synonym for "virtue," one we often use to describe what someone does. For example, we might say that a person is an excellent physician, or an excellent CEO, or an excellent parent.

However, the Greek philosopher Aristotle shines a different light on the concept, suggesting "excellence" or "virtue" is not only about what we do, but who we are. In this way, Aristotle draws our attention to character, which is something we are born with but also something we shape through our actions.

The "excellent" violinist has innate potential, yet she has spent years actualizing and developing that potential through practice. Likewise, a person's character is shaped by what they do. The choices we make and the actions we take become habits over time.

2

More than anything else, our habits express our character. Habits that promote our well-being while also fostering the well-being of others are called virtues. In contrast, destructive habits are called vices. Unfortunately, we all know people whose personal and professional lives have suffered because of bad habits.

Virtuous leaders are those who habitually make choices contributing to the well-being of the people, organizations, and communities they lead. Such habits include practicing the virtues described in *The 9 Virtues of Exceptional Leaders*—humility, honesty, courage, perseverance, hope, charity, balance, wisdom, and justice.

> **More than anything else, our habits express our character.**

While perhaps not an exhaustive list, we believe those are, at the very least, an excellent place for leaders to start.

PRACTICING VIRTUOUS LEADERSHIP TODAY

Are you a virtuous leader? Pick one of the Nine Virtues to focus on today. Write it down and post it in a place that will remind you frequently of the virtue (for example, next to your computer's display). Make it one of your goals to intentionally express this virtue through what you say and do throughout the day.

LISTENING EMPATHETICALLY
(humility)

The reason most leaders do not listen empathetically to others is because of pride.

One of the hallmarks of humility is a willingness to listen to others. Even then, either we listen merely to the words people are saying or we listen deeply and productively in order to understand what we are hearing.

One of the best ways to truly understand others is to incorporate empathy into our listening. Empathetic listening means connecting both with what the other person is thinking AND with what they are feeling. Put yourself in their shoes. Try to understand their experiences. Aim to share their emotions and comprehend their motives, passions, worries, hopes, and commitments.

Listening with empathy requires that we care about the other person and believe they have value.

When we listen empathetically, we hear more than the words people say. Listening with empathy requires that we care about the other person and believe they have value. This is the exact opposite of pride, which is a preoccupation with oneself and one's own achievements, knowledge, and possessions. This preoccupation with self inhibits our ability to empathize with another.

To lead virtuously, you must set aside your pride and focus on the well-being of others as you listen to what they have to say.

PRACTICING HUMILITY TODAY

Commit yourself to listen deeply to those with whom you engage. Concentrate on keeping eye contact during conversations. Try to listen more than you talk. Ask more questions than you usually ask, not only to gain new information but to understand what others are thinking and feeling.

HONESTY IS THE RULE
(honesty)

A reputation for honesty is perhaps the single most valuable asset any professional, and especially any leader, can possess.

Ironically, honesty is the virtue that most often becomes a target for exceptions. Can we expect anyone to tell the truth all the time? In times of war, lying is part of the game. If your spouse or significant other dons a hideous garment, should you tell the truth when asked how it looks? Can a small or misleading falsehood not prevent minor issues from becoming major ones?

Sometimes not telling the whole story or merely saying that you cannot or will not comment is appropriate. The philosophical dilemma that arises when virtues collide—for example, when what is charitable conflicts with what is honest—is real. (Consider the physician who, wishing to instill a sense of hope in the patient, does not reveal the full prognosis.)

Nevertheless, we should not exploit such exceptions to create a new rule. Leaders may lie to those who follow, but usually over time lying catches up with them. If people know that the leader is dishonest, credibility disappears—and with it goes the ability of the leader to influence and guide others.

If the people whom you lead do not know whether to believe you, they will always act cautiously.

If the people whom you lead do not know whether to believe you, they will always act cautiously, with distrust, and without commitment. This can breed animosity in the relationship. Truth-telling—old-fashioned honesty—is the rule.

PRACTICING HONESTY TODAY

Make honesty in your interactions with others your practice today. If you are in a situation in which you are unable to tell the whole story for whatever reason, practice honesty by saying you cannot (or will not) supply complete information.

ON FACING DIFFICULT DECISIONS
(courage)

Making decisions is the responsibility of leadership...

Nothing happens unless leaders make decisions. A decision is a choice to take one action as opposed to others—even if that means maintaining the status quo.

Some decisions are easy and need little or no input from others. Decisions that have a significant impact on an organization's revenue, employees, or customers, however, require a substantial gathering of data as well as the input of collective wisdom from those who have a stake in the outcome.

Leaders regularly find themselves in situations where rational analysis fails to yield the best direction, where risk reigns.

After all the information has been gathered, the most difficult decisions are those in which there is no clear answer. Leaders regularly find themselves in situations where rational analysis fails to yield the best direction, where risk reigns.

In response, we might put off making the decision, hoping the situation will resolve itself through other intervention or just go away. Letting a decision go unmade for too long can lead to more significant problems. Usually, a problem will not go away on its own but will fester and expand.

Thus, a leader must often make decisions, even when the solution is unclear. Making difficult choices—and being accountable for those choices—is the duty of leadership.

PRACTICING COURAGE TODAY

Consider a decision you have made that resulted in outcomes other than what you expected. Reflect on what you learned from that experience. How can you apply what you learned to make better decisions in the face of uncertainty? Consider having a conversation with someone you trust about your reflection.

DELAYED GRATIFICATION
(perseverance)

Perseverance is a matter of patience, of taking the long view.

Our culture does not favor the long view. It favors quarterly profits, a winning season, A's on the midterm and at the end of the semester, and overnight success. Impatience surrounds us.

Delayed gratification means resisting the temptation of an immediate, less valuable reward in favor of a more valuable one later. Studies associate the ability to delay gratification with many positive outcomes, including success in academics and business and benefits for our physical health and mental well-being.

> **We need the patience to see past the immediate reward and to persevere through failure to achieve something of greater significance.**

We need the patience to see past the immediate reward and to persevere through sacrifice, suffering, and failure to achieve something of greater significance. Unfortunately, many people have not given the long view much consideration. We sail through life, only thinking about one day of the journey at a time, without having a port or destination in mind.

For the leader, perseverance and patience need a compelling destination, a clear vision of the future.

PRACTICING PERSEVERANCE TODAY

As a leader, what is the long view for you? In just a few sentences, put it in writing. Consider if your destination is worth the time and effort to reach it.

EXCITING OTHERS ABOUT THE FUTURE

(hope)

The power of hope: to inspire others to see their world, their job, their role, not as it is, but as it could be . . .as it will be.

Every human being needs hope. Hope brings excitement and a feeling of expectation about a desired and desirable future. Hope brings encouragement and is the source of meaning and purpose.

The opposite of hope is despair. Hope is motivating; despair is paralyzing. Exceptional leaders understand that to make a positive difference in people's lives and the life of the organization, they must bring hope to those they lead. They do so through words and deeds that point toward a better organization, community, nation, and world.

When followers see that their leaders are animated by hope, they will also feel invigorated.

When followers see that their leaders are animated by hope, they will also feel invigorated. Exceptional leaders not only inspire followers with a vision, but they help followers see their place in this vision—their role in the future and the ways they can directly contribute to it.

PRACTICING HOPE TODAY

As you think about your role as a leader, identify a goal about which you are hopeful. Commit to talking about it today with your team or others who will be affected. When you speak, go beyond saying "I hope ...." Make your vision compelling by explaining why it is vital to the organization, how your listeners can become a part of it, and how they and others will benefit.

THE VALUE OF TIME
(charity)

Great leaders are generous with their time.

Whether considering the days of our lives or the hours in a workday, our time is limited. From our childhoods, we have been judged by how we use our time. It is not to be "killed" or wasted.

Indeed, time is perhaps the leader's most valuable asset. The demands on our time are constant, loud, and sometimes greedy. That others want your time is not surprising—after all, leadership is about accomplishing things through others. When you accept the role of a leader, you accept that those you lead will want your advice, access to the resources you control, your connections, and your support—all of which consume time.

Moreover, as a leader you commit to developing others. Thus, the tax on your time is a contribution you make to mentor and guide others toward achieving organizational, professional, and even personal goals.

The challenge is to find a balance: Great leaders need to use their time wisely, and they must protect time — for their organizations and themselves. However, they can also express generosity by being available on a regular and predictable basis.

Practicing the virtue of charity means that you look for opportunities to give your time to others who need it.

Practicing the virtue of charity means that you look for opportunities to give your time to others who need it.

PRACTICING CHARITY TODAY

Take 15 minutes and sit down with someone in your organization, a person with whom you do not talk often. Ask questions about how their work is going. Listen. Ask if there is anything you can do to help them.

A METAPHOR TO PRIORITIZE OUR LIVES
(balance)

Balance . . . is a lifelong pursuit.

Humans are the only living beings who are driven by nature to transcend their limitations. Our reach, as Robert Browning wrote, always exceeds our grasp. We dream, we have visions, and we set expectations that continually push our limits. Progress depends on this drive that is hardwired within the human species.

For some individuals, that drive is relentless. Indeed, many of us have become leaders precisely because we are so adept at pushing the limits in order to achieve what others consider impossible or improbable. Frequently, this comes at a cost; the one achievement that often eludes leaders and other high achievers is any semblance of life balance.

Here is how we define balance: giving all areas of your life—career, family, health, social relationships, spirituality, intellectual growth—their proper place in the grand scheme of things. Simply put, balance is a matter of time and attention to priorities.

If defined this way, balance can only exist in the moment because priorities are constantly shifting. Balance is not a destination, and it is not a state you can ultimately

In the end, balance is only a metaphor to help orient us to what is important in life.

achieve. In the end, balance is only a metaphor to help orient us to what is important in life.

The first step and every subsequent step in the pursuit of balance is regular mindfulness about priorities, time, and attention.

PRACTICING BALANCE TODAY

Mindfulness about priorities, time, and attention needs reflection. Take a few minutes today and reflect on the various areas of your life. Chances are you will discover an imbalance. Pick one area and identify one action you can take over the next week to improve in that area.

CURIOSITY IS THE
JOURNEY OF A LIFETIME
(wisdom)

*Lifelong learning is the first, indispensable, step toward
becoming wise.*

Our minds need knowledge just as our bodies need nourishment. Aristotle stated this truth in a few words with the very first sentence of his book *Metaphysics*, writing that "All [people] by nature desire to know."

Exceptional leaders are curious people. They love to learn, and they have many interests.

He offers as evidence the delight we have in the sense of sight, how we use sight to experience the world, distinguish among things, and, by our very nature, learn about how to survive and thrive.

However, as he points out, our senses alone are not wisdom. While they serve as conduits for knowledge of specific things, they do not tell us the "why" of anything. There is a difference between knowing facts and understanding why things are as they are.

Gaining wisdom is an ongoing process, one that never ends. Exceptional leaders are curious people. They love to learn, and they have many interests. They make connections between and among different fields, disciplines, and experiences to create innovative ideas and an exciting vision of the future.

This lifelong learning is not only about the external world, but also about self. Exceptional leaders are also on a lifelong journey of self-discovery.

Wisdom combines self-understanding and understanding of the external world (including others and subject matter) to result in practical actions that promote the well-being of other individuals, oneself, and one's community.

PRACTICING WISDOM TODAY

Challenge your curiosity today. Read something needing no more than 30 minutes of your time from a different field or business. A newspaper or magazine is a perfect place to find an article outside of your usual reading. As you read, look for something interesting. Look for a connection between this reading and some aspect of your personal or professional life.

JUDGE WITHOUT BECOMING JUDGMENTAL
(justice)

One of the leader's primary tasks is to make judgments—not only about issues but about people as well.

Leaders often make judgments about the organization's most valuable assets—people. Such judgments do not mean that the leader is judgmental, but that he or she is charged with making decisions that directly affect others and the organization.

Because exceptional leaders mobilize and motivate others to achieve visions and goals, it is vital that they recruit the right people into the organization and assign them to the appropriate functions. We usually hold leaders accountable for the decisions their subordinates make, even if they had little to do with those decisions.

Thus, leaders must regularly make judgments about whom to trust, in whom to invest time and money, and what level of responsibility is appropriate for various individuals and groups.

The leader's primary responsibility is not to himself or herself, nor to any other individual, but to the good of the organization.

Occasionally, the leader must decide to let someone go, as unpleasant as that may be. For a variety of reasons, not everyone will be a good fit for the organization's purpose. In making such decisions, exceptional leaders are guided by fairness, which includes being impartial, honest, and informed about those they lead.

PRACTICING JUSTICE TODAY

Consider a team that you lead or some individuals who directly report to you. How well do you know them? You are, after all, trusting them to get things done under your leadership. Identify two or three people (a manageable number for this exercise) and list what you perceive as their strengths and weaknesses. As you think about projects or goals ahead, write down how you could use these strengths—maybe in new ways—to accomplish what is ahead. Again, thinking about future projects and goals, make another list of potential blind spots these individuals have. How can you help them develop in these areas so that they become more effective at what they do?

We usually hold leaders accountable for the decisions their subordinates make, even if they had little to do with those decisions.

LEADING AUTHENTICALLY
(virtue)

For the best leaders, the behaviors most often associated with good leadership are authentic, not contrived; they are learned in the deepest and truest sense of the word.

We define "authenticity" as congruence between who you are and what you say and do. We once asked a group of leaders to state their values. One replied, "My values as they are or my values as I say they are?"

The question was an honest one, revealing the incongruence he felt. The disparity between his actual values, what he truly believed, and those he expressed represents a conflict of inauthentic leadership. Authentic leadership requires deep learning about ourselves—periodic self-examination followed by re-alignment of our goals, values, and behaviors.

We can also look to others for help maintaining our authenticity, as sometimes it requires another perspective to help us realize that we are acting in a way that is incongruous to our character—or to the character we would like to portray.

Virtuous leadership combines the act itself with the motivation behind the act to create a sustainable way of living. The behaviors of a virtuous leader are not contrived but instead arise from conviction, an overarching desire to do what is right for others, the organization, and the community.

Virtuous leadership combines the act itself with the motivation behind the act to create a sustainable way of living.

That is leading authentically.

PRACTICING VIRTUOUS LEADERSHIP TODAY

What are your values? Are your values virtuous—that is, do they promote the well-being of self and others? In your work today, find the occasion to discuss how one of your values (for example, service to your customers or students) is vital to the team or organization you lead.

THE HEALTHY EGO
(humility)

Becoming a leader at all without having a healthy ego is hard. You have to believe that you have something to offer, that you have worthwhile ideas.

Humility does not mean self-effacement. A virtuous leader can have a healthy ego and remain humble.

A healthy ego is rooted in self-awareness, including a knowledge of your strengths and weaknesses and an appreciation for what you have to offer. A healthy ego is the source of confidence, resiliency, and feelings of worth.

There is no one quite like you.

One way of developing a healthy ego is to reflect on your own uniqueness as a human being and as a leader. There is no one quite like you. You bring experiences, knowledge, personality, skills, and interests that no one else possesses. The combination of these variables is what sets you apart from others.

Getting in touch with what you uniquely bring to an organization, community, and those you lead is the first step toward making a positive difference that only you can make.

PRACTICING HUMILITY TODAY

Make a list of three to five things about you (upbringing, experiences, education, or other) that contribute to your unique style of leading. Beside each, make a few notes about how you can use these attributes to lead more effectively.

HAVING TRUTHFUL CONVERSATIONS WITH YOURSELF

(honesty)

Ultimately, the most important person to whom you must tell the truth is yourself.

Self-deception is the denial or rationalization of facts, evidence, or logic that run counter to our desires. Effective leaders aim for objectivity and avoid undue influence from those desires as they look for the good of the organization.

However, telling the truth to yourself is more difficult than it might appear. Our beliefs are propositions, and these propositions form the components of a constant dialogue in our minds, an internal conversation with ourselves.

Many of those conversations are habitual. A cue triggers them, and an internal discussion begins about a person, a set of circumstances, our work, or many other things. These conversations are how we think.

Because our ways of thinking become habits, we may come to believe many things that are not true, especially about others and ourselves. Telling the truth to yourself requires you to pay attention to the internal conversations, stop automatic responses that prejudge others, and challenge negative ways of thinking about yourself.

> **Our beliefs are propositions, and these propositions form the components of a constant dialogue in our minds, an internal conversation with ourselves.**

Being honest with ourselves means taking responsibility for those internal conversations and holding ourselves accountable.

PRACTICING HONESTY TODAY

Listen to your internal conversations. What are you telling yourself about others, about your job, about yourself? If you hear an untruth, reframe the discussion into a true one.

AGAINST PLAYING IT SAFE
(courage)

Sometimes playing it safe is the greatest risk of all—and the greatest source of regret.

Risk exposes us to the possibility of loss. In some circumstances, that loss may be multifaceted: reputation, money, credibility, and future opportunities. When leaders take risks, not only do they put themselves on the line, but others are also affected by their success or failure.

Given that making a risky decision often has significant and lasting effects, playing it safe is a common default. Yet if Julius Caesar had played it safe, he would never have crossed the Rubicon. The civil rights movement is replete with leaders, such as Dr. Martin Luther King, Jr., who risked everything for human dignity. Men walked on the moon only at enormous risk to themselves. Women's suffrage came about because Susan B. Anthony and others took not only political but also physical risks.

The history of leadership is a narrative of risk-takers who

28

both succeeded and failed. Taking a risk requires courage, the ability to overcome the fear of failure and loss. Courage, like the other virtues, develops over time and through experience. There is no magic formula for knowing when to take a risk, but the leader who declines to do so is not innovating and is not positioning the organization and its people to thrive.

> **The history of leadership is a narrative of risk-takers who both succeeded and failed.**

Moreover, for the leader who habitually plays it safe, the virtue of courage degenerates into the vice of timidity. Such leaders are apt to look back, after it is far too late, and wonder what might have been.

PRACTICING COURAGE TODAY:

Identify a situation that could, potentially, have a significant positive impact—but one where you have played things safe. Identify the specific risk involved and what is keeping you from taking that risk. Re-assess your position and consider what could happen if your risk-taking is successful.

PUTTING FAILURE INTO PERSPECTIVE
(perseverance)

This is what virtuous leaders understand: as long as they are striving, as long as they are moving forward, failure is not an end but merely a means.

Failure is part of life. As we learn to walk we stumble and fall over and over again. Researchers estimate the failure rate for new businesses is as high as 80 percent. Nearly every great leader has experienced his or her share of failures—Henry Ford's first company went bankrupt, 12 publishers rejected J.K. Rowling's first Harry Potter novel, and Oprah Winfrey was fired from her first job because she was deemed unfit for television.

For the exceptional leader, failure is always a means and never an end.

While no one likes to fail, what counts most in the face of failure is attitude. How will we see the failure? A failure is a mistake—we were wrong about something or someone was wrong about us. However, failure is also an opportunity to learn—about ourselves, about others, and about life.

For the exceptional leader, failure is always a means and never an end. Seeing failure as a means requires that we persevere through our mistakes—and those of others. We might continue toward the same goal as before, but with a different strategy. We might pivot, recognizing that what we were trying to achieve needs reframing and modification.

Alternatively, in the face of failure, we might even abandon the goal for a completely different one. Regardless, we continue to move forward. Virtuous leaders know that they can fail without becoming a failure.

PRACTICING PERSEVERANCE TODAY

What is your attitude toward failure, both your failures and the failures of those you lead? Take a few minutes and write answers to the following questions:

- When is failure acceptable?
- When is failure unacceptable?
- What are three or four lessons from my failures as a leader I can apply to decrease the risk of failure in the future?

VISION IS A FUNCTION OF HOPE
(hope)

Vision is an outer manifestation of a deeper virtue. It is another function of hope.

From the steps of the Lincoln Memorial, Dr. Martin Luther King, Jr. proclaimed these immortal words: "I have a dream that one day this nation will rise up and live out the true meaning of its creed—'we hold these truths to be self-evident: that all men are created equal.'"

Dr. King's vision echoed that of the leader in front of whose statue he stood. In his second inaugural address, Abraham Lincoln stated: "With malice toward none; with charity for all; with firmness in the right, as God gives us to see the right, let us strive on to finish the work we are in; to bind up the nation's wounds; to care for him who shall have borne the battle, and for his widow, and his orphan—to do all which may achieve and cherish a just and lasting peace, among ourselves, and with all nations."

Lincoln's and King's visions were vast—and both changed the course of a nation. Those visions occupy us still because they tap into a well of hope, not just for a different future, but for a radically better one. They are powerfully motivating visions, resonating so deeply that thousands gave the ultimate sacrifice to see them become a reality.

A compelling vision pushes the boundaries of what is possible.

While none of us is likely to encounter the dire prospects that Lincoln and King faced, and we may lack their oratory skills, exceptional leaders are frequently called upon to create a compelling vision of the future.

Such a vision gives people hope, a reason to carry on in the face of challenges that might otherwise seem insurmountable. A compelling vision pushes the boundaries of what is possible.

PRACTICING HOPE TODAY

Begin the process of radically re-envisioning your business or organization. Make a list of three to five things that push the boundaries. Schedule some focused time in the next month to develop a new and exciting vision that will motivate those you lead to face and overcome new challenges.

CHOOSING CHARITY
(charity)

Charity…is a rational choice.

The word "charity" is sometimes used synonymously with "love"; thus, we often associate the virtue of charity with how we feel. As leaders, however, charity is fundamentally about what we do—not how we feel.

Indeed, given that actions often follow emotions, charity sometimes requires that we act contrary to how we feel. What charity demands of leaders is that we give of ourselves to others. Leaders often must provide time, resources, guidance, and attention. These are valuable assets to all leaders, making their offering that much more charitable.

Charity sometimes requires that we act contrary to how we feel.

For a variety of reasons, expressing charity can sometimes be difficult. A leader may feel that the receiver of the gift is ungrateful; time and circumstances become impediments; occasionally, like anyone else, the leader may not feel generous at the moment.

Charity is a choice because exceptional leaders separate themselves from emotions and circumstances to assess rationally what is the right action regarding others. For virtuous leaders, right action is always aimed at what fosters the well-being of those who follow.

PRACTICING CHARITY TODAY

Identify someone toward whom you do not feel particularly charitable. Consider how you might help that person better achieve his or her potential. Choose to give something—your time or other resources—to create an opportunity for this person to grow and contribute more effectively to the organization.

HOW TO ASSESS LIFE
(balance)

Balance is about being fully aware in the present.

What do we mean when we talk about living a balanced life? If we mean a life without problems, then we will never achieve balance. If we are giving every part of life its due, such that every priority is in order and we are living in a state of perfect equilibrium, then we have achieved immortality—or something close to it.

Our mortal lives never cease to present new challenges. We are continually juggling our needs and desires, the good and the bad. That is life. A person may be at the top of her game at work, but physical exercise goes lacking. Focused time with family means time away from other social engagements.

What you perceive as balance represents an assessment of your life, and usually that assessment is not farsighted enough. During any given day, week, or even month, your priorities may seem to be in disarray. You are frustrated and pulled in many directions. However, extend the time frame to a few months, a year, five years. How does your life look now? In many ways, we cannot assess a life until its very end.

At any given moment, if you are paying attention to what matters, you are in perfect balance. Think of a time when you were with your spouse, significant other, or child and time seemed to stand still. At that moment, you were exactly where you should have been, doing what you should have been doing. That is balance.

Balance is a pursuit aimed at aligning the various dimensions of our lives. Are you pursuing it?

Balance is an ongoing assessment. How do you view the extended timeline of your life?

Ultimately, balance means living in the moment. Are you appreciating the joy of being where you belong, with the people who are important to you and doing the things that matter in the very moment of being there?

PRACTICING BALANCE TODAY

Identify a priority—perhaps a relationship with a loved one. Determine an action to take today that engages you in that priority. Once you are engaged, experience the flow associated with being exactly where you should be, doing what you should do. Focus your mind on the here and now, not on the past or the future.

PRACTICAL WISDOM IS ACTION ORIENTED
(wisdom)

Leaders are judged primarily by their decisions.

There are different ways to think about wisdom, but where leadership is concerned, the type of wisdom that is most essential is what Aristotle called "practical wisdom."

Practical wisdom goes beyond knowledge to understanding. Practical wisdom includes analyzing, evaluating, creating, and acting. Decision-making is the nexus between wisdom and action. It is the mechanism by which leaders move themselves, others, and their organizations.

Usually, we evaluate leaders based on the decisions they make—or avoid. Listen to what we often say of leaders: "He made a bad decision"; "She listens to others when she makes a decision"; "He just can't make a decision"; and so on.

All decisions are future-oriented; just as we cannot know the future, we cannot know in advance the outcomes of our choices. However, exceptional leaders are those who consistently make wise decisions.

Such wise decisions require knowledge of people and subject matter, experience (including the leader's experience and the collective experience of others), and emotional control—ensuring that emotions, ranging from fear to confidence, inform but do not override careful reasoning.

PRACTICING WISDOM TODAY

One way of becoming wiser and making better decisions is through reflection about what has worked and what has not worked as a leader. Consider a significant decision you made that did not go well. What are two or three things you can learn from that situation? Now consider a significant decision that had desirable outcomes. What are two or three things to learn from that experience? Now make a list of criteria to help you make better, wiser decisions in the future.

> **Decision-making is the nexus between wisdom and action.**

DIFFICULT DECISIONS, DIFFICULT CONVERSATIONS
(justice)

People are much less likely to believe they are being treated unfairly if they have some input into the decision-making process.

The virtuous leader treats others fairly, but fairness across an organization is an exceedingly tricky standard for at least two important reasons.

First, the leader usually makes decisions for the collective good. Often, what is good for the collective is not so good for certain individuals, even if those individuals are among the most loyal employees.

Second, fairness does not always mean treating everyone exactly the same. If two people have the same position in an organization and the same level of responsibility, then fairness means treating them the same in terms of resources, expectations, rewards, and other factors necessary for them to succeed.

However, if two people have significantly different respon- sibilities—that is, they are unequal in their duties—then the just leader must treat them accordingly. A manager who over- sees a division, a large staff, and a multimillion-dollar budget is treated differently, within the context of the organization, than an entry-level employee.

Most organizations are not democracies. Leaders are often called upon to make tough decisions, and among the most dif- ficult are those that affect the future of others within the or- ganization. Sometimes, when such decisions arise, leaders are tempted to avoid hard conversations with those who may suffer negative consequences.

That is when dialogue between leaders and others in the organization is most important. Fairness demands that leaders communicate—in good times or in bad.

PRACTICING JUSTICE TODAY

How would you rate yourself regarding fairness? Is there an awkward conversation you have avoided because you fear you might be accused of unfairness? Make the effort today to ex- plore justice with those who report to you. You might think of a significant decision you have recently made and ask if they believe they had appropriate input into the decision. You might think of an upcoming decision and ask for their opinions.

LEARNING TO LEAD
(virtue)

Lifelong learning is not merely the acquisition of facts; rather, it is the active desire to understand both the world and our individual and collective place in it.

Only at its most basic level is the purpose of learning to acquire or even retain facts. Learning—especially learning to lead—is really about the application of knowledge, not just its acquisition. Its ultimate goal is what the ancient Greeks referred to as "practical wisdom."

The universe never ceases to present us with mysteries to solve, questions to explore, and the unfathomable to appreciate.

Curiosity is a necessary condition for learning over a lifetime, since one must remain inquisitive—asking questions of self, others, and the world. The universe never ceases to present us with mysteries to solve, questions to explore, and the unfathomable to appreciate. All we have to do is look for them.

Exceptional leaders are continuously learning, and much of that learning extends beyond a job or discipline-specific knowledge to an understanding of the big picture and one's place in it. Asking deep questions orients each of us to our life's purpose and meaning in a way that is not merely philosophical or religious, but highly practical. This helps us stay focused on what is essential in life.

Those questions never end—but that is what makes life (and leadership) interesting.

PRACTICING VIRTUOUS LEADERSHIP TODAY

Put into writing a big question of importance to you. Commit to taking 15 to 30 minutes today to explore that question through reading, conversation, or quiet contemplation.

OTHER-CENTEREDNESS, NOT SELF-CENTEREDNESS
(humility)

There is no question that it is to your advantage to become less self-centered and more other-centered.

A certain amount of self-interest is natural and even healthy. Self-interest motivates us to learn, to exercise, and to advance in our careers.

However, leaders must move beyond self to others—the people and organizations they lead. They cannot become self-centered. To center on something means to make it your main focus of interest. Self-centeredness, then, involves putting yourself first, making your interests primary, and placing your needs and desires above those of others.

The words a person uses are a good sign of self-centeredness. If you find that your conversation is usually about you—what you have done, where you are going, what is important to you, or even what is not working so well in your life—then there is a good chance you are self-centered.

You cannot lead others if, as a leader, you are only thinking about yourself. A distinguishing characteristic of virtuous leadership is a concern for others. To center your attention on others means to make them your main subject of interest.

> A distinguishing characteristic of virtuous leadership is a concern for others.

Putting others first gives you the desire and ability to understand the people you lead, which is necessary if you hope to motivate and mobilize them toward a higher purpose and goals.

PRACTICING HUMILITY TODAY

Pay attention to your conversations today. Are they self-centered or other-centered? Listen especially to the pronouns you use. Do "I," "me," and "my" dominate?

PRINCIPLE-CENTERED LEADERSHIP

(honesty)

The trustworthy person is distinguished by consistency. This attribute involves having a guiding set of bedrock principles that remain unchanged because they are a part of your core being.

We can define "principle" in a variety of ways. It is a fundamental idea, a rule, or a guideline. There are many principles, but the ones that count most are those by which we live. These principles are commitments to ourselves and others to live and act in certain ways.

Principles, even if we are not fully aware of them, are the bedrock upon which we establish our families, our communities, and our organizations. While all leadership is shaped and influenced by the context in which it occurs, principles keep us consistent across changing situations.

Exceptional leadership is principle-centered leadership, not situation-centered leadership. If we lead based on the potential vagaries of our situations, we cannot establish trust. Trust requires that others have confidence in us regardless of circumstances, and such confidence demands consistency of behavior.

It sounds paradoxical in an age when we place such high value on free thinking and innovation, but exceptional leaders are predictable. Followers can rely on (or trust) them to act in ways consistent with the core beliefs that shape their attitudes and thus define their philosophy and approach to leadership.

It sounds paradoxical, but exceptional leaders are predictable.

PRACTICING HONESTY TODAY

Honest leaders are worthy of trust because they act consistently based on bedrock principles. For virtuous leaders, those principles promote the well-being of others and the businesses and organizations they lead. Make a list of the principles that guide your leadership. Pay attention to how you practice them—or when and why you deviate from them.

LEADERSHIP, RELATIONSHIPS, AND CORRECTION

(courage)

Correction is an absolutely indispensable part of leadership.

Leadership involves a relationship, but not usually a relationship among equals. That is, leaders have more resources, more positional power, and more autonomy to get things done. They also have more accountability.

Because leadership is a relationship, virtuous leaders seek healthy, positive, and even genial interactions with those they lead. Such interactions make us feel good—and they make those around us feel good as well.

At the same time, because leaders must accomplish things through others, they are stewards of the organization's assets—human, financial, and political. They are also the chief visionaries, moving the organization toward a

Because leaders must accomplish things through others, they are stewards of the organization's assets.

goal. If anyone in the organization is using its assets unwisely or exhibiting attitudes or behaviors misaligned with the purpose and objectives of the organization, then the leader has a responsibility to correct.

Providing constructive but critical feedback is difficult. It could result in conflict. Fear often leads to avoidance of conflict, yet leaders must possess the courage to overcome their fear and discomfort in order to have those difficult conversations when necessary.

Correction is merely an essential responsibility of leadership.

PRACTICING COURAGE TODAY

Is there an awkward conversation you need to have? If so, develop an approach that is issue-focused, respects the other person, provides an opportunity for that person to be heard, gives them clear guidance about expectations, and then is checked with appropriately probing questions to make sure they have registered your feedback.

WHAT KEEPS YOU AWAKE AT NIGHT?

(perseverance)

Few have the capacity for suffering that leadership requires.

During conversations with leaders, a question we often ask is, "What keeps you awake at night?" While answers vary, every leader to whom we have posed this question has a ready response. Moreover, what keeps a leader awake one night is likely to change the next night, or week, or month.

Leadership, as we have noted before, involves a relationship, and sleepless hours often result from thinking about how to address people problems. Leaders must also make difficult decisions that affect not only individual employee's careers, but also the lives of those connected to the employee—colleagues, families, and friends.

Also, leaders in most organizations must "manage up," and every leader is accountable to another leader (such as a board, stockholders, or stakeholders) or a client. Because all these relationships are different, people problems always include an element of uncertainty. Leadership can be a lonely place. The psychological suffering that leaders experience includes anxiety, stress, fear, and alienation.

Anyone who accepts a leadership role must have the ability to withstand psychological suffering.

Anyone who accepts a leadership role must have the ability to withstand the psychological suffering that is part of the responsibility. Sleepless nights come with the job.

PRACTICING PERSEVERANCE TODAY

What keeps you awake at night? Having mentors, advisors, and others with whom you can talk confidentially can help ameliorate the sense of loneliness. Talk with someone you trust and who has relevant experience with an issue you are facing. Resolve to act on the issue.

AGAINST THE CYNICS
(hope)

What if the opposite of optimism is not pessimism, but cynicism?

The famous Cynic, Diogenes of Sinope (412- 323 BCE), is said to have walked around Athens with a lamp he held to the faces of Athenians he met in his quest to discover an honest person. Plato allegedly referred to Diogenes as "a Socrates gone mad."

The Cynics were champions of virtue, but they are also the source of our current use of the term cynicism, the belief that self-interest alone motivates people. If we assume that people are so self-interested, how can we trust them to act on behalf of the group or organization?

> A leader cannot lead without trusting others, and others will not follow if they do not trust the leader.

A leader cannot lead without trusting others, and others will not follow if they do not trust the leader. Cynicism stalls progress. In contrast, exceptional leaders are confirmed optimists, eternally hopeful about the future and confident in the people who will create that future. That does not mean they deny reality. Instead, they practice the virtue of hope in their attitudes and behaviors, no matter the circumstances. Hope motivates people—including themselves—to act.

Exceptional leaders overcome cynicism with optimism and hope as they engage those they lead, develop them, create opportunities for them, and trust them to achieve goals that move the entire organization forward.

PRACTICING HOPE TODAY

As a leader, do you tend toward optimism or cynicism? Make it your aim today to have an attitude of hope and to use language expressing optimism when confronted with an uncertain or even potentially negative outcome.

AUTHENTIC LEADERSHIP
(charity)

The essence of authentic leadership is recognizing what you uniquely have to offer as a leader.

A finalist for a senior leadership position asked her mentor what she should do to prepare for the interview.

The mentor paused and, after thinking, said, "Everyone who is a finalist is qualified. You all have the experience, the education, and the drive. You all will arrive at the interview well studied, knowledgeable, and conversant with the latest data, trends, and financial projections. You will know a lot of the individuals and groups who interview you. So, my advice to you is to discover what you bring to this position that no other leader on the planet brings. Discover what is unique about you and allow that uniqueness to come through in how you present yourself. There is only one you—only you can bring your gifts to this job. That is what will distinguish you from the others."

The finalist followed her mentor's advice, was offered the

position as a result, and accepted. Authentic leadership requires being charitable to oneself—what we describe as healthy self-love. Moreover, love of self means recognizing, appreciating, and expressing your unique gifts as a leader.

PRACTICING CHARITY TODAY

Authentic leadership requires being charitable to oneself

What makes you different? What do you bring to your leadership that only you can? Think of your life experiences as well as your aspirations. Describe in a few sentences your unique way of leading. Identify an opportunity today to allow that uniqueness to shine for the benefit of others.

BALANCE DEPENDS ON LEISURE
(balance)

Leisure can be hard work!

To understand the meaning of leisure, we must return to the father of virtuous leadership, Aristotle.

Today, we think of leisure as play or pleasure, but for the ancient Greeks, leisure was considered hard work. The Greek term for leisure is *scholé*; the Latin derivative is *schola*. Most people recognize these roots as the origin of our word school.

Leisure is a uniquely human activity. Humans are *homo sapiens*: we are the wise (sapient) ones. Our rationality is central to leisure because reason allows us to engage in activities in which other animals cannot, such as friendships, spirituality, lifelong learning, family, politics, and reflection.

Leisure activities are those things we should do by virtue of our humanity. For example, we should be good friends to others, we should be involved parents, and we should continue to learn throughout our lives. As leaders, we should care for those we lead.

Some things are biological necessities, like eating and sleeping. While leisure is not necessary in that sense, it is morally obligatory because it is rooted in the core of our humanity. For that reason, balance depends upon leisure more than anything else. To use leisure wisely is to pursue balance.

Balance depends upon leisure more than anything else.

Being a good parent is difficult. So is being a good friend. So is leading others. Leisure is hard work—but it is essential work. Without leisure, we cannot live fulfilling—which is to say, balanced—lives.

PRACTICING BALANCE TODAY

Make a list of your leisure activities and identify the activity that, if you increased or improved it, would bring you greater fulfillment, more balance. Identify one step you can take today to give more time and attention to expanding this activity in your life.

THE BEST TEACHER
(wisdom)

Mentoring others is the wise leader's ultimate responsibility.

Everyone knows the adage that "experience is the best teacher." When we look at organizational leaders, this bias toward experience is clear.

While there are phenomenal exceptions to this rule (and most are genuine "phenoms"), CEOs, presidents, and educational leaders tend to be older. There is an optimum age, somewhere between 50 and 60, for people to assume the highest levels of leadership in their careers. Forbes reported in 2015 that the average age of a Fortune 500 CEO was almost 57.

C-Suite aside, in most hiring decisions, experience usually trumps education, other credentials, and personality. Think about how much experience has taught you. How much of what you have learned could only have come from experience?

If experience is the best teacher, then those who truly learn from their experiences become sages over time. As a leader, you also have a responsibility to pass on those hard-earned lessons. The people you lead can learn not only from their own experiences but also vicariously through yours.

Consider the difficult lessons you have learned through trying experiences. How much pain could we have avoided if someone who had traveled a similar path had passed along their wisdom? What if you had had a mentor to help you work through the difficulty?

If experience is the best teacher, then those who truly learn from their experiences become sages over time.

Whether you had that or not, you can do it for those who follow. As a leader, you must accept your responsibility to mentor others so that they can learn from your experience.

PRACTICING WISDOM TODAY

What are the most valuable leadership lessons that experience has taught you? Write them down. Now, develop specific steps you can take to help those who report to you understand and apply these lessons. Look for teachable moments when the lessons you have learned can be used at once by those you mentor.

JUSTICE, THE OUTWARD LOOKING VIRTUE

(justice)

Justice requires that we consider the needs of all, not just our own.

Not all leadership is virtuous leadership. Sadly, examples abound of leaders who are motivated by self-interest, whose aim is personal profit or the benefit of a few at the expense of many, or who show little concern for those they lead. We find such leaders in every community.

Justice is the defining virtue of virtuous leadership because unlike the other virtues, justice is outward looking. Justice has meaning only as it relates to others.

Virtuous leaders exhibit justice through their concern not only for their own well-being, but also (and primarily) for that of others.

Justice is the defining virtue of virtuous leadership.

Fairness is one way that virtuous leaders show justice. Fundamentally, fairness means giving each person his or her due. It includes impartiality, honesty, and freedom from favoritism or prejudice. Fairness defines transactional leadership: the leader and those who are led exchange things of value such as money for work, time for establishing a business relationship, or recognition for philanthropy.

A more profound expression of justice, however, is found in transformational leadership. Transformational leaders engage people in a higher purpose—the mission, vision, and values of the organization. They transform those they lead by helping them achieve their human potential through service to others. That is the best way to lead people—and the most just, because it is the most beneficial to all concerned.

PRACTICING JUSTICE TODAY

We might say justice as transactional leadership is about money, while justice as transformational leadership is about meaning. Considering those you lead, identify one person and engage them in a conversation about work—what they like about the job, what they would change if they could, and what keeps them coming to work. Listen to determine if the motivations are primarily about money, meaning, or both. In that conversation, ask if there is one action you could take to help this individual experience more satisfaction in their work. To the extent that you can, commit to take that action.

IT'S NOT ABOUT YOU

(virtue)

Virtuous leaders do not only learn to lead, they assist others along the same path by setting a good example, creating a learning-centered environment, and encouraging others both to learn and to lead.

One of the greatest lessons of leadership is that it's not about you—it's about others. It's not about getting what you want; it's about helping others get what they want. Once leaders recognize this, they are on their way to becoming virtuous.

Are you actively reaching out to others to give them courage?

There are three outward-looking "E's" of virtuous leadership:

- Example—are others learning how to lead, how to contribute to the good of others, by observing you?

- Environment—are you creating an environment where people can grow, achieve their potential, challenge themselves to become better, and ultimately thrive?
- Encouragement—are you actively reaching out to others to give them courage, to strengthen them, and even to push them to higher levels of competency and achievement?

Practicing the three E's focuses your leadership on achieving results by enabling others.

PRACTICING VIRTUOUS LEADERSHIP TODAY

Identify one person whom you can encourage today through actions or words. Using "thank you" is a good start. Use your encouragement to help that person reinforce behaviors that are productive and to motivate them to further contribute to your organization.

ABOUT THE AUTHORS

N. Karl Haden, Ph.D. is a philosopher, an entrepreneur, and the founder and president of the Academy for Advancing Leadership (AAL), a strategic consulting and talent development firm in Atlanta, Georgia. Through AAL, he has worked with over 150 institutions and organizations and thousands of individuals around the world. He is the author of numerous articles and monographs on leadership and educational policy. He is also the coauthor, with Rob Jenkins, of *The 9 Virtues of Exceptional Leaders* (Deeds, 2015).

Rob Jenkins is a professor, keynote speaker, and author. As a regular contributor to *The Chronicle of Higher Education* and other publications, he writes frequently about leadership, communication and teaching and learning. His books include *The 9 Virtues of Exceptional Leaders* (with Karl Haden), *Welcome to My Classroom* (Kendall Hunt, 2018) and *Think Better, Write Better* (Kendall Hunt, 2019). He serves as a Senior Fellow at the Academy for Advancing Leadership.

Imagine if all your leaders had the opportunity to learn and practice virtuous leadership. What differences would that make in the daily and long-term success of your business or organization? The Academy for Advancing Leadership (AAL) offers a spectrum of virtue-based development options tailored to meet your specific needs.

To schedule 9 Virtues workshops, speaking engagements, and consultations, please contact the Academy for Advancing Leadership at info@aalgroup.org or 404-350-2098. More information about the 9 Virtues model of leadership is available at 9virtues.com.

CPSIA information can be obtained
at www.ICGtesting.com
Printed in the USA
FSHW011820211219
65213FS